wanderers, witch-talkers

poems by Najia Khaled

Copyright © 2016 Najia Khaled
ISBN 978-1-329-98502-5

"rencontre" previously published under the title "the city" in cahoodaloodaling Issue #10

title "neither pink nor pale" from "witch-wife" © 1917 Edna St. Vincent Millay

"Witchcraft is the recourse of the dispossessed, the powerless, the hungry and the abused. It gives heart and tongue to stones and trees. It wears the rough skin of beasts. It turns on a civilization that knows the price of everything and the value of nothing."

— Peter Grey, *Apocalyptic Witchcraft*

"[Witches are] the embodiment of a world of female subjects that capitalism had to destroy: the heretic, the healer, the disobedient wife, the woman who dared to live alone, the obeah woman who poisoned the master's food."

— Silvia Federici, *Caliban and the Witch: Women, the Body and Primitive Accumulation*

Contents

witch   6
rind   7
Christmas lights in London   8
fancy, fantasy   9
mandate of Heaven   10
blackberries, brambles   11
Hubble   12
poison of kings   13
Arabian Nights   14
delicate position   15
sonnet to sertraline   16
luxuria   17
skeleton   18
one for sorrow   19
possession   20
on irrationality   21
rewind   22
puppeteer   23
tumble dry   24
animal   25
rencontre   26
devotion   27
coefficient of fiction   28
faerie tale   29
neither pink nor pale   30
PSR J1311-3430   31
distance, difference   32
relapse   33
subject, object   34
black wires, or: ode to women of colour   35
solitude   36

hallowed ground   37
fathom   39
temperate   40
I am not yours,   41
anything at all   42
Vienna   43
pedicellariae   44
infamy of Crete   45
Eurydice   46
cosmology   47
I am a prophet and yet I am a god   48
the theatre   49
firebrand   50
seven 'Ajwa dates   51
rise and shine   52
albatross   53
glutton   54
interred   55
Hell is murky   56
retraction   57
perd(u)re   58
snake   59
fool's good   60
beggar   61
confession   62
hatchet   63
finis   64
Salem   65

witch

my magic
is a product of necessity— of
wicked, intrepid urgency—
of quiet, inspired
lunacy.

women like me
don't bother to rein in
our greed;
there can be no sin
in anything I achieve
with such artless
enchantment.

I reign in
my mythology, in every story
ever conceived:
stars blossom and seethe
under my feet.

rind

I want to pry you open
like an exotic fruit,
to sink my thumbs into
the give of you;

to split you wide

through a thick, stubborn skin,
a pit like a worm
in dark, fleshy earth.

I want you with the strange compulsion
of a curse.

I want you with the steady
ache
of starvation,

the patient swell of hunger
that I diligently nurse.

Christmas lights in London

the city seems to glow
bright copper,
a scandal in oil colours,
a luminous quivering waste
of fog and smoke:

the rush-and-tumble
of the stonework streets,
a double-decker bus like the belly
of a beast,

the glittering air
at the back of my throat.

a metropolis that trembles
in inky blue
and gold.

fancy, fantasy

this is my saline dream,
spilling up your seaweed legs
(distorted vision,
faerie dance):

you are my sugar and cream,
wildflower fantasies
and oolong tea—
breath that comes in purple steam.

mandate of Heaven

in the interim
there is nothing much to
lose.

between the fall of one empire

and the rise of the next
there is always
some spurious strain of hope,

a period of
warring states
between body and mind:

in these times
I am lying on the bathroom
floor

with my head at the sink
and my feet in the bath,
letting the water

figure out the balance

blackberries, brambles

there is a resentment budding
in my gut
as something from a swallowed seed.

it lies
dormant and deadly,
a steady outdripping of poison,
thick as a sap to be tapped,
to be harvested.

I fear it will overrun my
careful pruning,
will corrupt the soil it grows in
with its violent outshootings—
will turn every bit of me
into its grisly garden.

will make you feel
its sting.

Hubble

the space between stars
in the night sky,
an eyelash's breadth,
contains billions of whirling
galaxies, lightless regions,
breathless clumps of dark matter
and other unimaginable mysteries.

and this reminds me of you.

poison of kings

I could devour
the past two hundred years
like arsenic,

layer them on my skin
like wallpaper:
powder-white, absynthe-
green.

I could consume two
whole centuries,
mix them with chalk or

vinegar
to dull the sting,
to improve the complexion.

I could eat an entire era:
an age of turmoil,
triumph, and intrigue

down my gullet
like a palliative, like a
poison.

I can almost feel it
roiling about
in my stomach:

urgent and metalloid
as a nightmare, as
a waking dream.

Arabian Nights

perhaps we are both made up of
subtle mysteries,
arcane secrets that we press
into each other's palms

perhaps I possess a thousand and one
tiny luminations,
my skin a Moroccan lantern,
your face aglow with projected light

perhaps there is the blood of an
Uqba ibn Nafi within me
and I could make a conquest
of you

and perhaps I would try, but
empires have fallen for less
than the feel of your hand in mine

delicate position

morning dawns
headaching bright

and I feel I could
carve out the sun
with a spoon:

scrape a star
from the sky, fling a god
from his chariot.

I go back to sleep.

sonnet to sertraline

        you'll be my death in battery
acid—globules of poison brought to me
        in teaspoons and thimbles, with their
placid edges, upturned and waiting for
        you, commander, to give them their duty.
dispatch your soldiers, then: your ragtag team
        of trinkets, emboldened, fit to
snatch the air from underneath my fingers,
        mobilised as they are: give me
mouthfuls of doubt like mesmerisms of
        light, like swallowing heat—that which
pulls my chest further into itself with
        each draught. little by little, I'll break free.
        give it to me. give it to me.

luxuria

if your body is a temple
then I've spent hours
worshipping my own personal gods:

scorching you with
the idle fire in my palms,
another psalm I mean
to desecrate

skeleton

light sears
through the chinks in her arched,
regal back.

she is eyeless and smiling,
her ribs a gaunt prison,
her shoulders an altar
eaten by moss.

there is a stark silent
dignity in the splay of her thighs,
in the crown of her head—
in the way that she lies there

and will not be turned to dust.

one for sorrow

I've got a kind of magpie magic
that I cultivate
whenever you're around:

peculiar and fanciful,
my familiar,
my own self.

I swallow superstitious horror:
omen, portent,
harbinger:
I safeguard stolen
scraps of silver.

I revel in your evangelism.

I am a charm,
a mischief,
a murder:

a tiding
all on my very own.

possession

how much of you do I own

the crescents between
your fingers
, the inflection of your voice,
your opinions on Descartes
and physics and the
colour pink,

will you spill them into my hands
like red wine,
can I call them mine

on irrationality

I begin to think that I am
selfish, headstrong,
obstinately cruel:

ridiculous as a gardener
who stops tending
to a bed of flowers

only to be
shocked and grieved
when weeds begin to grow

rewind

I dreamt I was a necromancer,
dreamt I was a demigod
who resurrected cultures, peoples,
skin and teeth and bones and hair.

I dreamt I was a logician, clinician,
an imagined anthropologist,
a linguist tinged with dark,
dark magic:

drew dialects into my mouth,
reawakened languages,
undid a hundred hundred years.

but it's a heavy, pricey spell.
I take the weight of ages and ages.
the yokes of seven continents
clang upon my pale brown hands.

puppeteer

abandoned like a cart of flesh,
a pauper's hook on which to chew—
your iconography, your ruse,
that statue of you
with its claw and its root.

you will latch onto me
like a skin, you will split
me in two

and fill all of the crevices
with miniatures of you.

tumble dry

laundry day came
in a tumult of procrastination,
fingers worn as rags,
skin eggshell-white
and -dry

(pale porcelain with cracks
and freckles,
the heart a fleshy yolk,
yellow with jaundice
and indecision)

and a chore as mundane
as folding linen
became a metaphor,
fertilised and fit for
breaking open

animal

you cajole me with hundreds of mouths,

a roar and a screech and a hiss and howl;

something hideous, something foul
that lurks, nocturnal,
outside my window. / that wakes me up

with a piteous growl.

rencontre

these are the things I leave behind:
love like a headstrong art,
a barrage of skyscrapers lined up
like battleships,
a strange, surreal cityscape
with furtive alcoves and concave places
in which I hid my secrets.

perhaps one day I will
walk these streets without
stringing regret along at my heels—
I will greet the weeds
that struggle through the concrete
like lovers.

devotion

I adore each thing
you've touched,
separately—I afford
to every object
its due reverence.

you left your fingerprints
on a glass yesterday
and I touched each
impression in oil,
one after the other,
an offering in miniature,
a phantom kiss.

over a smear of lipstick
you've left on a spoon
I ghost my lips.

coefficient of fiction

in the morning
I am monumental.
my body is a half-
dream, a Goliath
of form,
before the sun rises
to dwarf it.

in this bleary light,
I can be anything.

faerie tale

falling out of love with you
was like awaking from a dream:

dizzy and bleary-eyed,
gorged and oversoaked
with sleep.

I'd eat a dozen
poisoned apples, drink any measure
of liquor,

prick each finger
on every spindle I could find

for another year, twenty,
a hundred
of that enchanted death.

but the spell is up.
I am no princess, and there is no war
for me to slumber through

other than my own.

neither pink nor pale

I am luminescent in patches and strings,
full bursting heavy with gluttonous weeds;
a witchy abundance of small deadly things;
trailings of light like clutters of beads.

I am resplendent in tatters and rags,
nor holy nor wretched nor fallow nor fair;
a desolate wonder of caverns and crags;
glories of skin and messes of hair.

I am magnificent in carpets and furs,
a classical marvel of marble and oil;
perfumed and heady with incense and myrrh;
bright and conflagrant with trouble and toil.

I am incandescent and ancient and rare.
I am the sorcery that sorcerers beware.

PSR J1311-3430

this is how I quantify
your remove
from me: ladders of

cosmic distance,
angles of
inclination,

our minute
stellar parallax.

you, my standard candle,
pulsar heart,
the scale by which
I measure everything:

you are bright and beautiful and
unaffected, and I

am left to ponder
the geometry
of longing.

distance, difference

you are a fever dream
and I am a benediction

I bubble up from the mouths of saints
and hiss and gleam in your
warped vision

and I am the wasp sting
to your honey, I am contrition

relapse

this, I think,
is the way that empires
fall.

there are sometimes
catastrophes—
Vesuvius, Alexandria—
but I will not go out
in such an explosive fashion
this time.

my second death
is preceded by decline,
slow and inglorious;
erosion working its
weary charm
upon my architecture.

someday, archaeologists
will discover my ruins
and sigh.

subject, object

for someone so passionately
against animal cruelty
you've never had a problem
experimenting
on people.

you won't touch a chicken's egg
for anything
but you fucking
vivisected me

black wires, or: ode to women of colour

I don't have skin like ivory–
no roses bloom within my cheeks–
I blush in livid, vivid blue.
deep bloodshot violet. / a sickly
hue.

I don't have breasts like driven snow–
no flaxen fields wave in my hair–
I rush in amaranthine pools.
deep, bloodshot, violent. / an oath,
a due.

solitude

chipped bone china,
two lumps of sugar,
enough blackberry rooibos tea
to drown in
(if one is very determined)—
a silver service arranged
gleaming and precise
as a skeleton.

one day, the silence
of this house
will have drunk me
to the dregs.

hallowed ground

i.

Heaven is not a place for
wanderers, witch-talkers,
women with words
between our teeth—

we purveyors of sinister
magic, we perpetrators
of wicked misdeeds.

we who are muck and mire
and marrow,
stuck hollow to the soil beneath
our feet—

we whose blood bubbles thick,
arcane, and dark.
we with candlewick tongues.
we with cauldron hearts.

ii.

ours are the whispers
that seethe in the streets;
ours are the fires
and the sinkings of stones;

ours the desires
that brew and that breed;
ours the rebellions,
ours what we've sown.

ours are the murmurs
that churn in the dark;
ours the disquiet
and ours the alarms;

ours the awakenings
in glyph, lynch-pin,
charm.

rabbitfoot, lionheart,
we cultivate harm.

iii.

I have become enamoured
with pain.
with sickness and rot.
with the roilings of rage.
with things we can wield.

I have become enchanted
by sorrow.
by illness, unrest.
the things we can conjure.
the things we've worn best.

I am in love
with the magic that nestles
inside of my breast:
infirm and unmotherly,
mine and my own.

cold as a witch's teat,
dry as a bone.

fathom

and since you asked,
yes, this is how
I always see you:

grinning, unchaste,
eyes a
bright toxic viridian,
like a bowlful of
Mediterranean sky;
like an ocean

sliced open at the
meridian,
baring its frigid depths,

each tentacled squid,
each sucker and fin and
poisonous thing,

parted for me
as if I were Moses,
as if you were the Red Sea,
as if I could see

every wild thing
that teems within you

temperate

spring is not the gentle unfurling
of feeling, the shuddering growth
of the blossoms of May,
that it once was. this year, it is

an explosion of unregimented hope,
a violent uprising of sentiment—
resplendent and raw
and fierce as an April thunderstorm.

I am not yours,

though I would like to be:

would like to be
(not drowned,
only eclipsed in an
onrush of tidal structure)
yours,
in the least binding
sense of the word.

would like to
lose
at least part of myself in you.

but I can find in you
only a cadaver, ghastly and immaculate:
white as a wedding gown
and more pristine.

anything at all

I am the answer,
I am fronds of fire,
I am dire, pure, religious
awe:

I am a dirge beat out on
bells, beat out on
sticks,
beat out on the naked swell
of my thighs:

I am golden, molten,
shimmering, I am my
tongue and I am my
skin,

I am a roped-off room
to die in.

I am a small copper pot
full of sin.

Vienna

their dead never crowded
my mind,
I never lurched beneath
the weight of
too many bones
that were not mine:

rather, a kind
of hesitant symmetry
began to overtake
the place,
to invade every narrow space
where, previously,
a doubt had been.

I've been wrong,
all this time:
they are not storming
my fortress,
assailing what is invulnerable.

rather, they are laying
siege—
waiting for the inexorable
pull of hunger
to break me

just enough

pedicellariae

I am not a street
urchin
I am a sea
urchin

spikes and venom and
bristling
with mystery

but everyone seems to call me
by the wrong name

infamy of Crete

the past year plays on repeat in my mind,
insistent, stereoscopic.

I think of how you used to love me
and it makes me sick.

I walk with the light at my back
so I can scan the shadows for your form,
those iron shoulders, those lofty horns.

I do not need a ball of string.

the labyrinth itself unwinds
beneath my feet, shifts at my back,
get away, you beast.
get away, you beast.

Eurydice

you keep secrets like souvenirs;

your heart a postage stamp,
your lungs a pair of dusty
snow globes. I trace

a model Eiffel Tower
in the lines of your neck, an Arc
de Triomphe in the arch
of your back, a collection of
portraits

to rival the Louvre
assembled beneath your brow.

I gather each glimpse
of the things you've tried to hide

and hoard them
in the galleries of my mind,
curating my love for you
like a dense, Orphic art.

cosmology

I'm running out of lofty ideas.

you are a veritable Arcturus,
a supernova,
red giant,

but I can't find the words
to fuel your fusion:

I am a black hole
where light buries itself.

I am a prophet and yet I am a god

oh, but this suffering is a sacrament!
lying backwards off of the bed,
arms outstretched in a parody of piety,
in paroxysms of guilt!

oh, but the absurd mirrors the sublime!

this scene is ridiculous as it is
religious:
the buzzing of fluorescent lights
in my blood, in the skin of my teeth—
the only scourge upon my cheek
mascara
and not pox or plague.

and yet, a holy hush descends,
as if I am hallowed!
as if I am blessed!

Jesus of Nazareth had skin like mine—
Muhammad spoke the language from which
I draw my name—
my bones are the bones into which
Al-Quddus blew life!

oh, but I am a portent of the Divine!

the theatre

it is a Tuesday afternoon
and I observe
the proscenium arch
of your spine.

I am separated from you
by several degrees,
a world and a half,
the ornate, sweeping divide
between watcher and watched

(and you've never cared
to break the fourth wall)

firebrand

I hope you burn yourself
on the words
that I've given you.

I hope the soft skin
of your fingertips
bubbles up

with heat and wanting,
a thousand petty thieveries
of syntax.

I hope you can never touch
anything
ever again

without thinking of me.

seven 'Ajwa dates

I have the claws of a gargoyle
and the mouth of one, too.

I, siren's screech,
harpy's scream,

scold, spit-fire, shrew.

I she-witch,
shawafa
with my oil and lead.

I termagant,
torturer
with my hatchet and screw.

I with the skin
of a snake.
I with the maw of a beast.

I with the will of a jinni
and the fire of one, too.

rise and shine

daybreak is a vial
of liquid amber
spilt out against the sky

when I wake up.
there is enough warmth
between us, I think,
to coax the very sun
into existence—

the press of you
against my back, the
swell of you
within my chest,

the breath and motion
of people like us,
drowsy in our crowds
of blankets.

you stir behind me,
and it blinks
its bleary eyes.

albatross

I've swallowed everything

but still I wake reeling,
heavy and beleaguered with longing
to wrench,
giddily free,
from corset-lace, stick-pin,
deadweight anchoring me
leaden
to the bedpost.

glutton

I want to throw you to the ground,
throw you to the wolves,
devour you whole in an agony
of teeth:

I'd take you in my tea
like sugar, like cream—
I'd take you on the ground
like a wild thing, like a beast.

I'd split my lip
trying to swallow you whole.

interred

death like a sycamore,
its black, black railings,
shakes like a root
in my girded heart:
its bars tremble
something terrible.

I fear that I am
guarding some black art,
spectral desire,
witchcraft urge:
with a grim compulsion
I rattle my fastenings.

Hell is murky

you're dark as plum juice,
heady as a wound—

an ink-violet stain
that blooms
in the pool of my throat,

red, red wine
that purples on my skin
like a bruise.

blunder-you, blemish-you;

arcanest mark,
indelible scar.

surest, sweetest sorcery
that ripens in my mouth
like fruit.

retraction

and what do I title this interaction:
gasping and idle,

your spine curved up on the end
like a question,
your body indelible?

I want to blacken both my eyes
with your slackened fists,
with smudges of make-up,
with nothing more

than the suggestion of your name

perd(u)re

I loved you
as I am going to lose you:
steadily, and without artifice.

like the clearing of floodwaters.
like the healing of a wound.

there is something within me
that does not permit permanence,
something rancid inside
that slowly wears through—

I cannot keep. I lose. I lose.

but I am determined, this time,
to do it gracefully: to make it
a skill that I can perfect,

a performance that commands awe,
a sideshow of precious things
slipping through my fingers.

somewhere, behind a curtain,
on a rickety platform
surrounded by strangers,

I am losing you
as I have loved you:
willingly, and without reservations.

with the depth of an ocean.
with the tenderness of a bruise.

snake

I will slough off
all my feelings for you
like a second skin
for somebody else
to slip into

fool's gold

an early September afternoon
and summer's drunk down
to the dregs,
golden and lukewarm.

this is the first year in six
that I've allowed myself
a sip, then several long swallows
of daylight,

my skin darkening until it seems
I have a facsimile of sun
in each pore.

it is not yet too cool
for a fine sheen of sweat
to gather on my arms—

in the shifting light of the season
they glitter like pyrite.

beggar

I am not a stumbling-place,
a pole for your crooked heart to climb.

you couldn't love me any more
if my words were ruts
meant to grab your wheels,
could you?

I didn't construct my castle
just to receive your stones
at the windows

confession

If I could, I wouldn't hesitate
to feel
the heft and heat
of everything inside of you;

I'd ferret out
your sins,
I'd sell indulgences, I'd sew
coins
into the lining of your skin.

hatchet

I am an ocean of sound,
a black roiling graveyard:
I suck at your ankles
with a smirk and a *pop*.

you can feel my lungs,
heavy illustrious machines,
in the tow beneath your feet
and for a second I think I
have you.

but you open your mouth
in a foreign tongue, displaying
the message, the martyr, the faint
hypocritical twinge;

a lopsided carnival
rioting along your teeth.

I reel back my waves
with a gasp.

finis

I wasted a year of my life,
so many outpourings of my heart,
love like a rind
down a garbage disposal.

I will grow a new year
from the stump of the old one.
I will grow a new heart
from the stone of the old one.

I will grow a new love
from the pit
of my stomach
and it will obliterate the old one.

Salem

I.

the bright scarlet egg of dawn
nests in my head.

when it is time, it will crack my
skull like a shell
and be born.

II.

I have a witch's fingers and a
witch's eyes, rough pewter lenses
through which I see the world.

I have sabotaged their crops,
I have plagued their children,
I have eaten their livestock in the night
   (so they say)
and I hear the whispers in the streets.

they are willing to kill
for their conviction, though I
am not willing to die for it.

III.

I am no longer human.
I've been branded
with an ugly mark
of fear and desperation,

one terse syllable that cuts
like a switch.

IV.

a thin reddish line splits the horizon;
I set my ribs on hinges
so they can get to my heart.

a damp wooden platform,
a rough rope necklace—
I am not a Spartan
carried home on his shield.

this is not an honourable death.

About the Author

Najia Khaled is a Moroccan-American lesbian poet who is currently studying linguistics at the University of Rochester. She has been published by cahoodaloodaling and Word Smiths. This is her first published book of poetry.

contact: najiak1101@gmail.com

Made in the USA
San Bernardino, CA
26 April 2018